CALLED TO REIGN WITH CHRIST

CALLED TO REIGN WITH CHRIST

AUTHORITY AS STEWARDSHIP IN GOD'S KINGDOM

DANIEL GOMMA

HIGH BRIDGE
BOOKS & MEDIA

Called to Reign With Christ
by Daniel Gomma

Copyright © 2026 Daniel Gomma

ISBN: 978-1-962802-61-1

All Scripture quotations, unless otherwise indicated, are taken from the Holy Bible, New International Version®, NIV®. Copyright ©1973, 1978, 1984, 2011 by Biblica, Inc.™ Used by permission of Zondervan. All rights reserved worldwide. www.zondervan.com. The "NIV" and "New International Version" are trademarks registered in the United States Patent and Trademark Office by Biblica, Inc.™

High Bridge Books titles may be purchased in bulk for educational, business, fundraising, or sales promotional use. For information, please contact High Bridge Books via www.HighBridgeBooks.com/contact.

Published in Houston, Texas, by High Bridge Books.

"It is the glory of God to conceal things, but the glory of kings[1] is to search things out."

—Proverbs 25:2 ESV

"I tell you the truth, anyone who believes in me will do the same works I have done, and even greater works, because I am going to be with the Father. [13] You can ask for anything *in my name,* and I will do it, so that the Son can bring glory to the Father. [14] Yes, ask me for anything *in my name,* and I will do it!"

—John 14:12–14 NLT

"By his divine power, God has given us everything we need for living a godly life. We have received all of this by coming to know him, the one who called us to himself by means of his marvelous glory and excellence. And because of his glory and excellence, he has given us great and precious promises. These are the promises that enable you to *share his divine nature* and escape the world's corruption caused by human desires."

—2 Peter 1:3,4 (emphasis added) NLT

" '(...)And you will be my kingdom of priests, my holy nation.' This is the message you must give to the people of Israel."

—Exodus 19:6 NLT

CONTENTS

INTRODUCTION

WHAT IF THE GOSPEL IS NOT ONLY GOD rescuing sinners, but God restoring rulers—raising sons and daughters who bear His likeness and represent His reign? This book argues that Scripture's language of "Image," "Name," and "Kingdom" is not poetic decoration but a concrete vocation: to be formed into Christ's likeness through worship and union, and to exercise delegated authority under the true King. Yet such a calling is never merely inspiring; it is also sobering, because to be made in God's Image is to be entrusted with a real share in His purpose for the world—and to misuse that gift is to deform both self and creation.

It is both wondrous and fearful to be made in God's image and likeness: to share, as a creature, in His creative potency—and yet to live as though this cosmic reality were unreal. If I live as though I were merely matter and appetite—nothing more than impulse with a pulse—I will inevitably begin to mimic the nature of an animal: heeding urges, enslaved to whims, and sowing havoc by the way I think, speak, and act.

The fact is that we are inevitably endowed with a creative prowess made manifest by thought, word, and deed. Because God's gifts are irrevocable[1], our nature of being co-creators with Him was not repossessed nor diminished when we strayed away and ignored the fulness of our identity in Him. Knowingly or inadvertently, we continually create our existence through the unspoken words we nourish in our minds. Our original design carries a creative potency, so our thoughts act as seeds. What we nurture within eventually sprouts into words, and words mature into deeds— toward Life when in Him, or toward destruction when detached from Him.

Have you noticed how beliefs become destinies—how what we take to be true quietly governs what we attempt, what we refuse, and what we call 'possible'? The human condition is, simply put, divided between those who live in a perpetual, and therefore unfulfilled state of potential—hoping one day to become God's children and heirs to His Kingdom—and those who already share in His nature and daily choose to live in that state of fruition as image bearers: children of the One God above gods, Yahweh.

Once it sinks in that this astonishing Being speaks the truth in Scriptures—that any orphan who believes and accepts becoming His child has the option of fulfilling their identity in its entirety—then we understand that, like Him, we become co-creators through thought, word, and deed. Every thought we have is a seed that in due time sprouts into words, which in turn, matures into corresponding deeds.

That we are able to create chaos and destruction if we choose the paradigm of independence and orphanhood from our Creator is a startling thought. But, on the other hand, we are capable of creating a remarkable environment that gushes Life wherever we stand, if we daily choose to live according to His original paradigm.

This book unveils what it means to live as true bearers of God's very Nature, and how such a transformation unfolds in the life of a believer: we lay down every claim of entitlement, and God answers not with mere pardon but with sonship. Then He seals that sonship with His signet—marking us with His Name and commissioning us to act on His behalf. Thus we are summoned into a sobering and glorious reality as co-regents, exercising delegated authority under the King who is soon to return.

1

THE HIDDEN WAYS OF GOD

I WRITE THESE WORDS EARLY IN 2024, WHEN THE world seems to have forgotten how to wonder at what is hidden and tacit. We have grown impatient with mystery, uneasy with silence, reluctant to trust what moves beneath the surface. God often chooses to unveil His truth through clarity, but also through contrast—by letting light be glimpsed through inference. He remains the Master of discreet revelation, whose subtlety invites the soul to listen more deeply than the noise of the age allows.

In the various tacit ways in which God communicates, He also hints at His realities by portraying polar opposites, or, if you may, *indirect codes*. Those who learn to see that which is veiled are the ones who begin to understand the transformation He offers—becoming like Him through worship, aligning their hearts with His Son, and participating in His creative work.

For instance, there are numerous verses in the Old Testament pointing to the dangers of idolatry. Worshiping idols breaches the very first tenet in the Decalogue[1], also known as the Ten Commandments, and denatures the person who is fooled into that practice. Psalm 115[2] declares that those who worship idols will become like them, having eyes but not seeing, ears but not hearing, mouths but not speaking. In

Psalm 135³, we see the same dynamics. Together, these texts press one sobering reality upon us: we inevitably become like what—or whom—we worship.

Simply professing a religion won't fulfill us. Abstaining from specific sins won't either. Attempting to obey tenets and commandments won't cut the deal and will never complete the human being. However, worshiping our Father will make us just like Him, conforming ourselves to the image of His Son.⁴ This is where we find fulfillment.

Sonship is brought about by fulfilling our original calling—being one with Him through worship. Fulfilling our ultimate calling will inevitably make us like Him, conforming our being unto His very Being, taking His form and function. This is a profound revelation in both the written Word – Scripture, and the incarnate Word – Christ Himself.

This transformative power of worship is most fully revealed in Christ, who became man to bridge the gap between God and His children. Christ becoming a man was extraordinarily debasing for Him, but He submitted Himself to it in order to be the Mediator, the link that connects Yahweh to His children. At once, Christ looks both at us and at the Father. He is the Rock in whose cleft we hide to be nearer to the Father,⁵ just as Moses did in Mount Sinai. Through Christ, we've been rescued from eternal punishment, and those who acknowledge the debt and daily accept His unfathomable payment, now have God look upon them and say, "Ah, my beloved and flawless[1] one."

---

[1] "For by that one offering he forever made perfect those who are being made holy." Heb 10:14 NLT

A number of hidden and indirect codes are made available to those who can clearly see what qualifies us as God's children, His representatives and co-rulers in His Kingdom. Don't fret if it initially sounds startling, as it might as well be indeed. If you remember nothing else: God's hiddenness is not absence but training. Worship forms likeness. Likeness qualifies representation — and representation is the seed of regency. Are you ready to be stunned?

"Even before he made the world, God loved us and chose us in Christ to be holy and without fault in his eyes." Ephesians 1:4 NLT

"(…) and you are holy and blameless as you stand before him without a single fault." Col 1:22 NLT

2

ROYALTY AND REGENCY

REGALS HAVE LONG ENTRANCED PEOPLE—the pomp, the refinement, the influence, the elegance and aplomb. So many ostensible features have intrigued and drawn generations to look to royalty for inspiration. Is it the sense of exclusivity? The finesse? The clout? The power (be it tacit or factual)? Whatever the reason, something undeniable generates appeal to all, both young and old.

My family and I moved to London a few years ago, and something about being here has stirred my heart in unexpected ways. The language of "kingdom" feels less like a distant metaphor when you're living in a place that once shaped so much of the world—where, as they used to say, 'the sun never set'. And yet, royalty can still generate mixed feelings, drawing both affection and frustration.

That tension has made me wonder: if an imperfect, human throne can move people so strongly, what would happen if we caught even a glimpse of the true King and His Kingdom? I can't imagine anyone seeing that—really seeing it—and walking away unchanged. It seems to me that its reality, its beauty, and its worth would be beyond dispute.

And that is precisely where Jesus placed His emphasis. Jesus did not speak for (or against) any religion; He focused exclusively on the Kingdom of God. He desired to inaugurate something new with His parables and teachings and by the way He lived. He wasn't merely describing a distant hope—He was announcing something arriving in the present. The Kingdom of God was at hand, and the King Himself had come over for its inauguration.

And His announcement wasn't only an invitation to believe something—it was a summons to participate in something new. He was declaring a Kingdom that would advance in the world, and He intended to entrust its work to His beloved children who would represent His rule.

In this Kingdom, Jesus desires regents—those who govern on behalf of a king by delegated authority. God's invitation into regency is not born of absence or limitation; it springs from generosity: the Almighty entrusts His interests to His children.[1]

The ones God desires to appoint as regents are His children who fearfully accept the stunning invitation to rule with Him, on His behalf as heralds of His interests. However, those who still succumb to the temptation and deceit of believing that their value is not bestowed but earned cannot receive such regency. They still believe their value comes through service and is self-generated by attempting to tally up worth by acts of self-justification. On the other hand, God is ready to bestow His Authority onto those who are quick to acknowledge that only He is worthy. More on this soon.

Jesus repeatedly frames discipleship as an invitation into regency—participation in God's rule—by using parables that emphasize trust, stewardship, and restored authority. In the Parable of the Talents and the Minas (Matthew 25:14–30; Luke 19:11–27), servants are entrusted with their master's resources during his absence, and their faithfulness determines the degree of authority they receive upon his return, with commendation explicitly expressed in terms of governance: "You have been faithful over a little; I will set you over much." Likewise, in the Parable of the Prodigal Son (Luke 15:11–32), the repentant son is not merely forgiven but reinstated with symbols of rule and belonging—the robe, the ring, and the feast—signifying restored authority and sonship within the household. Together, these parables reveal that Jesus' call is not only about moral reform or personal salvation, but about forming faithful heirs who are trained, tested, and ultimately entrusted with real responsibility in the administration of God's Kingdom.

If Jesus' parables present discipleship as training for regency, then the Bible's persistent emphasis on justice clarifies the substance of that training. Throughout Scripture, God reveals himself not merely as a powerful king but as a Righteous One, whose rule is defined by justice, equity, and faithfulness to the vulnerable. A regent who governs in God's name must therefore reflect what is most central to God's reign. Justice runs like a central thread through the biblical story—from the Law and the Prophets to its complete and undeniable fulfilment in Jesus—because justice is what righteousness looks like when it becomes real in the world. To be entrusted with authority in God's kingdom is to be entrusted with the responsibility to uphold what God upholds, to set right what has gone wrong, and to order life in accordance with His character. In this light, justice is not a secondary concern but the essential mark of those who are being formed to share in God's rule.

3

JUSTICE

IN SCRIPTURE, JUSTICE IS NOT A MERE SOCIAL concern; it is God's holy order set right—His way of addressing rebellion and restoring creation.

The world runs on laws that existed long before we had the scientific language to describe them. We didn't invent gravity, thermodynamics, or mathematics; we learned to observe and articulate what was already factual. The same is true of electricity and electromagnetism: they weren't created by humanity but discovered as realities woven into the fabric of creation. In a similar way, there are laws that govern the spiritual realm. Whether we understand them clearly— or ignore them entirely—doesn't lessen their power or change their consequences in our lives.

From the beginning, God ordered creation and called the first humans to rule within it. Yet they chose not to abide, and they tasted the consequences of violating what is holy and true—sending a ripple through all their descendants. Adam and Eve inaugurated a world of consequential injustice, after lawlessness had already been inaugurated in the spiritual realms, thus perpetuating this paradigm through sin.

The then serpent, who enticed the first revolt, was so successful in continuing rebellious acts and became so well nourished by sin that it grew into the dragon[1] in Revelations. Yes, evil can be fed by our acts of rebellion, which expands the territory where God refrains from being present—namely, the empire of darkness. That happens not because darkness overpowers Light, but because He loves us so much and respects our free will to choose. Our bad choices create the only scenario in which darkness can 'conquer' Light. Through acts of rebellion, doors are open, giving legal authorization to spiritual beings of darkness to cause havoc on earth. Sinning is contracting an infinite debt, one that is unpayable. It enslaves the fooled party for life, for eternity. Unless we are bailed out by someone with infinite resources, we are doomed to remain forever slaves.

This is why understanding God's justice is essential: it is the mechanism by which the damage of rebellion is addressed, and true restoration is made possible. Justice is central in the spiritual world, and the ultimate Judge will bring complete closure to lawlessness at the appointed end. This process has already been initiated, and the eternal debt has been settled, but because freedom is the ultimate expression of love, we must first acknowledge our debt so that we can accept the eternal bailout. Yes, this is spectacular indeed.

When Jesus was faced with the rigid facet of first century religiosity, a main focus of His was to teach the Pharisees the insufficiency of their self-righteousness.[2] The only righteousness that can stand before God is God's own measure of righteousness—complete righteousness, a Shalom standard of rectitude. Any attempt to derive value from perceived personal expressions of righteousness is vain and deceitful[2].

Paul warned the believers in Rome not to misunderstand the mechanism of righteousness: it isn't wages paid out for good works, but the unearned result of faith. Righteousness is received as a gift—not something anyone can manufacture or claim as a personal achievement. Blessed, then, are those who don't consider themselves rich in their own righteousness, because they are already rightful heirs of the Kingdom.[3]

If justice is God's order set right, then the first disorder it confronts is not 'out there' but in here: the ego's attempt to justify itself.

We fall into believing we deserve this spiritual wealth whenever we measure ourselves against others. In that comparison, we inevitably see ourselves as either superior or inferior—and in either case, we're deceiving ourselves. This futile habit doesn't lead to clarity; it leads to self-absorption. The philosopher Martin Buber recognized this trap: when we live by comparison, we feed the ego[4], constructing an identity based on how we stack up against everyone else. The theologian Hans Urs von Balthasar went further, describing this self-focused life as an "Egodrama"—a narrative in which we cast ourselves as the protagonist of our own story, rather than characters within God's larger purpose.

The only escape from this self-centered entitlement is to lose ourselves in the Creator and His assessment of who we

---

[2] "For they don't understand God's way of making people right with himself. Refusing to accept God's way, they cling to their own way of getting right with God by trying to keep the law." Romans 10:3

are. When we do, we're invited into something far larger and more beautiful: the Theodrama—God's unfolding story of redemption and restoration, in which we are given real roles to play, not as protagonists of our own small narratives, but as participants in His grand purpose.

The Theodrama[5] is von Balthasar's term for God's active drama in history—His work of creation, redemption, and renewal. Unlike the Egodrama, where we're endlessly focused on our own standing and performance, the Theodrama relocates us. We become partners with God in His Kingdom work, our lives reoriented around His values and His vision rather than our comparative standing. This shift from self to service, from ego to participation in something divine, is both liberating and deeply purposeful.

And here's what makes this so encouraging: we're not condemned to live as chronic prisoners of self-obsession. There is a way out—a way that doesn't require us to manufacture our own worth, but to receive it from the One who created us and knows us completely.

4

GOD-GENERATED RIGHTEOUSNESS

EVERY GENERATION DEFINES VALUE IN ITS own currency—whether influence, social standing, wealth, physical prowess, or, in our current era, digital attention. For many first-century Jews, that currency was righteousness (both personal and communal) and its visible expression: justice lived out in all its forms.

The Jewish people had been called to a distinct way of life, separated from pagan nations. The Hebrew idea of the "holy" (*kadosh*) carries the sense of being set apart—separated for a devoted purpose—and this separation was meant to be fleshed out in thought, word, and deed

Yet that commitment was consistently tested, most notably when Jewish men intermarried with women from pagan nations[1]. These unions didn't simply blur cultural lines; they brought spiritual consequence, as wives who worshipped pagan gods drew their husbands away from covenant faithfulness. What seemed like a personal choice rippled outward, undermining the very separation that was meant to protect the community's allegiance to God and existence in Him.

There is a deep vein of moral and spiritual aspiration running through the Jewish tradition. I say this as someone with Jewish heritage. The wisdom accumulated over centuries is vast and precious. Such teachings guided countless generations giving them means to navigate challenging times and contexts. When I was younger, I encountered Joseph Telushkin's *Jewish Literacy* and was struck by the wealth of insights contained there, the accumulated knowledge of a people committed to seeking God's truth.[2] Every follower of Christ can access much beauty from our older brothers in faith, albeit we must keep complete dependence on Him throughout the process of pursuing and acquiring[3] wisdom. We'll explore this further as we continue.

Jesus dismantled the illusion of self-generated righteousness through His parables and teaching. He made clear that true righteousness—the cornerstone of God's Kingdom—is never something we produce or earn. True righteousness, one of the main tenets of the Kingdom of God is only God-generated, God-bestowed, and God-ordained. As we remain grafted into His virtue, we can exhale the pleasant perfumes[4] of this original source. As C.S. Lewis articulated so well, we are but "a scent of a flower yet to be found, a hum of a song yet to be heard."[5] We are the scent; Jesus is the flower. We are the humming; He is the song.

Cultural Currency

As generations express their own sense of value, they inevitably project such perceived qualities into their collectivity. Monetary wealth is one of the most obvious forms, but various cultures tacitly adopt different currencies. Some believe physical prowess is more valuable and will find a way to showcase their physical features manifest in every relationship. Others value academic achievements and will make sure to be known first by their academic titles and accomplishments. Others attempt to derive their sense of value by associating themselves with presumably valuable brands or by wearing gleaming accessories. The fact is that the human experience is unavoidably mendicant (begging for worth), and the sooner we realize that, the more prone to be blessed we will be.[6] We look any and everywhere for validation, for a sense of worth, but will rest only when eternal value is found—that prototypical measure filled to the brim.[7]

The religious leaders in Jesus' time dealt with this struggle. As mendicant as the next man, they did everything possible to be known as righteous, law-abiding citizens. There was a common desire to be identified as the righteous ones. However, our acts of righteousness are but filthy rags[8]—useless to the core if our motivation is to muster acceptance from others or from the Father.

Jesus' parables are saturated with this same theme. When the Master speaks of riches, there are many signs that He is pointing to an underlying, perceived sense of worth—not merely to financial wealth.

> "You say, 'I am rich. I have everything I want. I don't need a thing!' And you don't realize that you are wretched and miserable and poor and blind and naked. So I advise you to buy gold from me—gold that has been purified by fire. *Then you will be rich.* Also buy white garments from me so you will not be shamed by your nakedness, and ointment for your eyes so you will be able to see." (Rev 3:17,18 NLT emphasis added)

"For not knowing about God's righteousness and *seeking to establish their own*, they did not subject themselves to the righteousness of God." (Rom 10:3, NASB emphasis added)

"She has been *given the finest of pure white linen to wear*. For the fine linen represents the good deeds of God's holy people." (Rev. 19:8, NLT emphasis added)

"So I *advise you to buy gold from me — gold that has been purified by fire*." Could Jesus be referencing gold, the metal? No, He is referencing God's Holiness, which cannot be purchased in a transaction, but rather through relational worship and by actively trusting that trials are fully authorized by God in order to approve us[III].

Then He says to John, "Also buy white garments from me so you will not be shamed by your nakedness." White garments are attained solely by the Blood of Jesus,[9] which removes all blots, and prepares those in such attire to partake in the ultimate Wedding with the Bridegroom.

However, Jesus also says, "Buy from me … and you will be rich." So the Kingdom does involve a kind of transaction — just not a financial one. The currency is not money, but

---

[III] "I will bring that group through the fire and make them pure. I will refine them like silver and purify them like gold. They will call on my name, and I will answer them. I will say, 'These are my people,' and they will say, 'The Lord is our God.'" Zachariah 13:9 NLT

a trusting relationship; the cost is not coins, but one's heart, soul, mind and strength[IV].

Jesus portrays this exchange in the parable of the man who discovers treasure hidden in a field. Overwhelmed by the worth of what he has found, he sells everything he has in order to buy the field and secure the treasure[10]. The point isn't that God is selling salvation to the highest bidder; it's that the Kingdom is so valuable that it reorders a person's entire value system. When someone truly sees it, "everything else" becomes secondary.

In this sense, what Jesus describes is not a commercial transaction but a spiritual one: whole-hearted surrender. We "trade away" our grip on self-rule—our image-making, our self-constructed security, our private little kingdoms—so we can receive the life of the true Kingdom. And when that surrender happens, God never responds with a measured equivalence; he gives with an abundance that overwhelms anything we imagined we were offering. He is the ultimate over-deliverer.

Trying to be good doesn't cut it. Many evaluative adjectives, such as "good," can be subjective, because their meaning often depends on perspective or standard. Using them can sometimes imply comparison, However, if we were to compare our righteousness with that God's, we would be able to better see how this is an exercise in futility. God is not only perfect and perfectly righteous, but His ways and thoughts are also unfathomably more elevated than ours.[11]

IV "The man answered, "'You must love the Lord your God with all your heart, all your soul, all your strength, and all your mind.' And, 'Love your neighbor as yourself.'" "Right!" Jesus told him. "Do this and you will live!"" Luke 10:27,28 NLT

Jesus exposes this dynamic repeatedly in His teaching. In the parable of the rich man and Lazarus, for example, He reveals how easily a sense of moral "rightness" can be assumed—especially by those certain they are already on God's side—and the story is crafted to strike the ears of the religious in-crowd. The rich man reads his comfort and sense of belonging as proof of security, imagining that his worth has been accumulated through merit, achievement and even entitlement.

Because he occupies the socially and religiously privileged position of a "proper" religious man, he supposes he has acquired spiritual capital[v].

Lazarus, by contrast, has no visible resources with which to manufacture that kind of assurance; he cannot produce the markers the 'spiritually rich' man relies on, and so appears—by that logic—is spiritually destitute - stripped of any settled sense of safety.

In the moment of truth, they were both surprised. One thought he had accumulated enough righteousness and justice to eventually face the Supreme Judge, and the other was always ready to accept that he could not generate either and was therefore constantly on standby to accept any portion of justice he could obtain. He was spiritually, a beggar. Both figures in this parable, although they appear to be very different, had much more in common than one might imagine.

---

[v] "The temple of the LORD… the temple of the LORD… the temple of the LORD" in Jeremiah 7:4 is labeled "deceptive/lying words" in the passage, because it functions like a slogan: *we're safe because we have the building and the rituals*. Jeremiah targets reliance on sacred space as a substitute for repentance and obedience.

Both were destitute. However, one presumed to be affluent in the spirit and the other knew he was not.

This dissociated waltz of opposites populated Jesus' teachings.

Consider the contrast he draws in the prayer of the Pharisee and the tax collector:

"Two men went to the Temple to pray. One was a Pharisee, and the other was a despised tax collector." The Pharisee "stood by himself and prayed" with confidence in his own moral record—"I'm not like other people"—even listing his religious achievements: "I fast twice a week, and I give you a tenth of my income." But the tax collector "stood at a distance and dared not even lift his eyes to heaven as he prayed." Instead, he "beat his chest in sorrow" and pleaded, "O God, be merciful to me, for I am a sinner."

Jesus then delivers the reversal at the heart of the story: "I tell you, this sinner, not the Pharisee, returned home justified before God." And he seals it with the warning (and promise) that frames so many Kingdom reversals: "Those who exalt themselves will be humbled, and those who humble themselves will be exalted."[12]

Being conduits of God's virtue is exhilarating indeed. As we are transformed by His Mercy and exercise the unavoidable tenets in Scriptures, virtue will be a (super)natural outcome. The danger is believing we are able to somehow generate such virtue and justice ourselves. Yes, it flows through us, but it is not ours.

> [21] "I hate all your show and pretense—
> the hypocrisy of your religious festivals and sol-
>   emn assemblies.
> [22] I will not accept your burnt offerings and grain
>   offerings.

> I won't even notice all your choice peace offer-
> ings.
> ²³ Away with your noisy hymns of praise!
> I will not listen to the music of your harps.
> ²⁴ **Instead, I want to see a mighty flood of jus-
> tice,**
>
> **an endless river of righteous living."** (Amos
> 5:21–24 NLT)

The JPS translation of verse 24 states, "But let justice well up like water, Righteousness like an unfailing stream." Would we be able to generate a "mighty flood of justice, an endless river of righteous living"? I don't think so. We continually fall prey to drinking water from our own cisterns, instead of drinking from the living waters, springs that continually gush pristine waters.[13]

However, we can allow such floods of justice to flow through us and let rivers of righteousness gush through us. We just need to acknowledge this is not ours. We're merely earthen vessels carrying around this treasure of unfathomable value.[14]

Jesus said that rivers would flow from within us[VI], those who believe. This echoes the biblical river imagery, the concept of righteousness that flows in us, but is generated in the throne of God, where—amazingly—we are seated with Christ[VII]. When Paul says that we are already seated with Christ in heavenly places, and Jesus says that He would give

---

[VI] "Whoever believes in me, as the Scripture says, rivers of living water will flow from within him." John 7:38

[VII] "God raised us up with Christ and seated us with him in the heavenly realms in Christ Jesus." Ephesians 2:6

the victors the right to sit with Him on His throne[VIII] what does this mean? That Paul was already a victor—more than a conqueror[IX]—just as you and I are, if we remain in Him.

> "But thanks be to God, who in Christ always leads us in triumphal procession, and through us spreads the fragrance of the knowledge of him everywhere." 2 Cor 2:14 ESV

More than conquerors in Christ

In the first century, the concept of victory was strongly linked to the model of Roman triumphs. These triumphs—one of which is recorded on the Arch of Titus—were ceremonial parades in which the victorious general was led in a quadriga, followed by the spoils of war and the humiliating procession of defeated enemy officers, often displayed on floats[X] that illustrated their capture, as narrated by Flavius Josephus[XI]. The triumphs involved drinking and feasting and culminated at the temple of Jupiter, where animals were sacrificed in abundance. The general—*triumphator*—then had his presumed apotheosis, being treated as a god—at

---

[VIII]] "To the one who is victorious, I will give the right to sit with me on my throne, just as I was victorious and sat down with my Father on his throne." Revelation 3:21

[IX] "But in all these things we are more than conquerors through him who loved us." Romans 8:37

[X] Such as those seen at the *Sambódromo* in Rio de Janeiro, during its world renowned Carnaval.

[XI] Book 7 of "The Jewish War" by Flavius Josephus.

least for that day. In this case, father and son—Vespasian and Titus—celebrated their co-triumph.

Christ's triumph involved something similar, but much more glorious. On the true Via Sacra, and not the Roman one, He and the Father paraded the spoils of His conquest—all these supposed deities were exposed to eternal shame on the Cross, even though at that moment they were convinced that they had defeated the Undefeated One. The moment Christ expired, the Father tore "His garments" in the temple, from top to bottom, and the object of His Love—you and I—have not an *apotheosis*, but a *theosis*[XII] in Him. Now free to worship Him unhindered, we gradually become like Him, with Him. The more we recognize that only He is worthy, the more He dignifies us. Today, because of Christ, we are elevated to an authority greater than that of the countless simulacra of gods on display — all much greater than you and I, but **much** smaller than the One who dwells in us. This tireless God insists on inviting us to be transformed, newly and definitively into His image and likeness, daily and gradually, fulfilling the ultimate theosis as we worship Him forever and ever, one day at a time.

Experiencing such theosis does not make us ontologically immaculate like God while on earth, but rather, it inducts us into a dialectical existence in which we join in His Holiness. While sharing His Nature, we still bear scars, and yet we become conduits of His healing.

[XII] Theosis is participation in the life of the one true God, while apotheosis is elevation to godhood. Theosis preserves the distinction between the uncreated God and the created child; apotheosis erases it. In theosis, only God is worshipped; in apotheosis, the deified human becomes the object of worship.

Like Japanese art of repairing pottery with gold—kintsugi[15]—our Healer, Yahweh Raphah, mends our brokenness, making us co-agents in His healing process for others who experience similar imperfections, cracks, and wounds.

In such dialectical existence, we, although unable to generate righteousness on our own, become bearers of the Perfect Righteousness of God. Here, we are invited to witness courtside His magnificence meeting brokenness, redeeming the world of those who are led to a position where they can choose Him.

The prophets Jeremiah and Isaiah, both remind us that true wisdom, righteousness, and justice come from God alone.

> "This is what the Lord says: "Don't let the wise boast in their wisdom, or the powerful boast in their power, or the rich boast in their riches. But those who wish to boast should boast in this alone: that they truly know me and understand that I am the Lord who demonstrates unfailing love and *who brings justice and righteousness to the earth*, and that I delight in these things. I, the Lord, have spoken!" (Jer. 9:23-24 NLT, emphasis added)

> [10] I delight greatly in the Lord;
> my soul rejoices in my God.
> For he has *clothed me with garments of salvation*
> and *draped me in a robe of his righteousness*,
> as a bridegroom adorns his head like a priest,
> and as a bride adorns herself with her jewels.
> [11] For as the soil makes the sprout come up
> and a garden causes seeds to grow,

*so the Sovereign Lord will make righteousness
and praise spring up before all nations.* (Is 61:10–11)

Saul was unwavering in his abilities to generate his own righteousness until he met with the Christ on the road to Damascus, was "draped in a robe of righteousness," and had his metrics of value fully reassigned, now as Paul. It's hard for us to grasp how competent, well trained, and privileged[16] Paul was. On top of that, he was a Roman citizen. But when he met with Christ, the real source of all Virtue and Wealth, Righteousness and Justice personified, he could then speak with such propriety about the incomparable Nature of God through Christ.[17]

> [1]"Is anyone thirsty?
> Come and drink—
> even if you have no money!
> Come, take your choice of wine or milk—
> it's all free!
> [2] Why spend your money on food that does not
> give you strength?
> Why pay for food that does you no good?
> Listen to me, and you will eat what is good.
> You will enjoy the finest food.
> [8] "My thoughts are nothing like your thoughts,"
> says the Lord.
> "And my ways are far beyond anything you
> could imagine.
> [9] For just as the heavens are higher than the
> earth,
> so my ways are higher than your ways
> and my thoughts higher than your thoughts."
> Isaiah 55:1,2,8,9 NLT

5

THE ESTATE OF LIFE

JESUS WAS (AND STILL IS) CONFRONTED WITH THE pervasive paradigm of self-merit in a nation that had to live and excel amid pagans whose worship and ethics often ran contrary to covenant life. Jews were commanded to keep themselves holy by staying separated[1] from the idolatry, sexual licentiousness, ethical ambiguity, and self-serving liturgy of the Greco-Roman and other ancient cultures. When they did, they flourished; when they succumbed to marrying their sons and daughters to those bound to pagan gods, they fell hard and painfully.

Even when outwardly successful in observing Torah, the danger was subtler: the heart's drift into self-congratulation—'holier than thou'. Justice and covenant love belong to the foundations of Yahweh's Kingdom and, therefore, are the highest treasure in the Bible. Justice is a pervading biblical principle that exudes from God, but thinking we can *repay* the Ultimate Giver is folly of the highest degree. Righteousness/justice (often expressed in the Hebrew concept of *tzedakah*[2]) could become, in practice, a kind of moral 'currency'—a way of tallying worth, by exercising the Mitzvot,[3] or the commands in Torah. Yet Scripture is unsparing about where that road ends.[4]

We are free to act righteously because He loved us first and redeemed us at the cross—where Christ completed what righteousness requires — so that His righteousness now **flows** through us, expressed in deeds done without self-display, as when "the right hand" does not announce what the left is doing (Matthew 6:3).

Uncovering the Hidden Treasure

Jesus often spoke in parables because it is the privilege of reigning regents (His royal heirs assigned to govern) to search out what God has chosen to conceal. Proverbs 25:2 says, "It is the glory of God to conceal things, but the glory of kings is to search things out." God often reveals Himself through what is hidden, and those who pursue Him with reverence will find Him.

On our own, we'd never be able to discover such treasure, which is why Jesus spoke about the Kingdom of Heaven as being a treasure trove found in a field.[5] The man in the parable, who sold everything he had, could barely afford the field—let alone the treasure itself. How tremendously fortunate we are. We have such a generous God who allows us to access the treasure by merely purchasing the land surrounding it.

Studying Scriptures is buying the field; finding God is opening the treasure trove. Diligently studying a matter is buying the field; God revealing the matter is finding the hidden chest. Practicing spiritual disciplines is buying the field; meeting with our Father is striking cosmic gold. Accepting Christ's redemption after repenting is buying the field; receiving Him and becoming subjects in His Kingdom is finding the hidden treasure. Becoming regents in the Kingdom of God is finding the motherlo— I mean, the *Fatherlode*.

And when that treasure is found, life changes. Regency is not the treasure; it is what communion produces. The treasure is fellowship; regency is its consequence. We buy the field with obedience, but God gives the treasure by grace—and from that gift flows a people made capable of faithful rule under the true King.

This is paramount for our understanding that:

1) Accessing Him, His Kingdom, His Authority and becoming His children is finding the treasure. All disciplines we exercise to reach the above are merely buying the field.

2) Once this sinks in, we are finally in a position to confess that we are not worthy in ourselves, and nothing we do can add to our ontological value. Christ has secured our worth by His blood and His triumph at the Cross.

3) Once we confess that *we are not worthy, even to be called His children*, then and only then does everything change, and we are ready to accept, receive, and exercise His authority on earth to expand His Kingdom. Remember Christ's admonition to say that "we are unworthy servants; we have only done our duty."[6]

Merit's Illusion and Grace's Reality

Jesus had to deal with many religious figures who thought they were "the last coke in the desert," as some say in Brazil. If they experienced God's favor, it was never by their own merit, but by grace.

In Luke 15:2, the Pharisees complained that Jesus associated with sinners and even ate with them.[7] Bear in mind the dynamics of judgment. If I consider someone impolite, it's usually because I deem myself as being polite. If I call someone uneducated, it's because I see myself as instructed or refined. If I allow my own perception of whichever trait to be the interface when interacting with someone else, that will be the standard through which I inevitably deal with that person. My interactions with them can be distorted, limited, scarcity-based, and unedifying.

Therefore, when Jesus heard that the Pharisees were dissatisfied that He mingled with sinners, what were they deeming themselves as? The word "Pharisee[8]" means "set apart" in Aramaic, which is the translation of the word *kadosh* (holy, set apart). So, they saw themselves as holy, set apart from those they deemed "sinners."

And it was precisely then that Jesus answered with the tryptic parables of the lost ones: the lost sheep,[9] the lost coin,[10] and the lost son. The latter, also known as the Parable of the Prodigal Son, is instrumental in portraying what takes place when one is finally ready to acknowledge that *all* value is in Him, and there is nothing we can add to that - ever.

The Parable of the Lost Son

[11] To illustrate the point further, Jesus told them this story: "A man had two sons. [12] The younger

son told his father, 'I want my share of your estate now before you die.' So his father agreed to divide his wealth between his sons.

¹³ "A few days later this younger son packed all his belongings and moved to a distant land, and there he wasted all his money in wild living. ¹⁴ About the time his money ran out, a great famine swept over the land, and he began to starve. ¹⁵ He persuaded a local farmer to hire him, and the man sent him into his fields to feed the pigs. ¹⁶ The young man became so hungry that even the pods he was feeding the pigs looked good to him. But no one gave him anything.

¹⁷ "When he finally came to his senses, he said to himself, 'At home even the hired servants have food enough to spare, and here I am dying of hunger! ¹⁸ I will go home to my father and say, "Father, I have sinned against both heaven and you, ¹⁹ and I am no longer worthy of being called your son. Please take me on as a hired servant."'
²⁰ "So he returned home to his father. And while he was still a long way off, his father saw him coming. Filled with love and compassion, he ran to his son, embraced him, and kissed him. ²¹ His son said to him, 'Father, I have sinned against both heaven and you, and *I am no longer worthy of being called your son.*'

²² "But his father said to the servants, 'Quick! Bring the finest robe in the house and put it on him. Get a ring for his finger and sandals for his feet. ²³ And kill the calf we have been fattening. We must celebrate with a feast, ²⁴ for this son of

mine was dead and has now returned to life. He was lost, but now he is found.' So, the party began.

²⁵ "Meanwhile, the older son was in the fields working. When he returned home, he heard music and dancing in the house, ²⁶ and he asked one of the servants what was going on. ²⁷ 'Your brother is back,' he was told, 'and your father has killed the fattened calf. We are celebrating because of his safe return.'

²⁸ "The older brother was angry and wouldn't go in. His father came out and begged him, ²⁹ but he replied, 'All these years I've slaved for you and never once refused to do a single thing you told me to. And in all that time you never gave me even one young goat for a feast with my friends. ³⁰ Yet when this son of yours comes back after squandering your money on prostitutes, you celebrate by killing the fattened calf!'

³¹ "His father said to him, 'Look, dear son, you have always stayed by me, and everything I have is yours.³² We had to celebrate this happy day. For your brother was dead and has come back to life! He was lost, but now he is found!'" (Luke 15:11–32, NLT emphasis added)

This story is laden with cultural nuances that highlight the outrageous, loving nature of the Father. In that world, a son asking for his share before his father's death would be a shocking act—publicly dishonoring his father and treating him as 'good as dead'. At best, he might be sent away and effectively disinherited. Yet the father responds with an almost unbelievable grace, granting him *his share* and letting him go

This is a pivotal point in the story. What the younger son received was exactly what he felt entitled to—*his share.* The Father gave the boy what he thought was indeed his—what he had amassed through his acts and his merit.

Remember when Jesus was speaking to hypocrites (Pharisees and scribes), drawing attention to their acts of righteousness? He said they had already received all the reward[11] they'd ever get.[12] The word for "reward" here is the same found in Matthew 5:12[13] in which Jesus speaks about our reward in Heaven. The contrast is sobering: a finite reward paid out now—applause, validation, reputation—versus an eternal reward received in due time is the very one which separates Life from death. This principle is reflected in the father's words in the story, when he says, "For your brother was dead and has come back to life! "

The estate of Life is the *Fatherlode.* The estate of death consists of the crumbs already handed out every time we do something for the show, to validate ourselves, or to be respected by the religious community. When spiritual disciplines become ends in themselves—tools for self-justification rather than means of communion—we begin spending those scraps immediately.

The estate of death is ravaged by the inflation of vanity and promptly evanesces. On the other hand, the estate of Life cannot be corroded by moths nor is it subject to economic fluctuations. It is gold refined by fire, unending, unfading, and unlimited.

> "You say, 'I am rich; *I have acquired **wealth** and do not need a thing.'* But you do not realize that *you are wretched, pitiful, **poor**, blind and naked.* [18] I

counsel you to buy from me gold refined in the
fire, so you can become rich; and white clothes to
wear, so you can cover your shameful nakedness; and salve to put on your eyes, so you can
see." (Rev. 3:17,18, NIV emphasis added)

It couldn't be clearer: the younger son's reward—the
crumbs he earned himself—is fleeting, while the Father lav-
ishes him with true riches, just as Revelation 3:17,18 describes: gold refined in the fire, white garments to cover
shame, and eyes opened to see. The estate of Life, the Fatherlode, far surpasses anything we could generate on our own.

Fleeting Rewards or the Fatherlode?

Because the prodigal son thought himself entitled, worthy of
such request, the portion he received wasn't his father's—it
was metaphorically the crumbs of righteousness he himself
had amassed through his finite acts of justice. Just like the so
called hypocrites, *he received his reward*. He squandered the
little he could wrap his mind around and eventually came to
his senses. Planning his speech, he headed back to boldly
plead to be accepted—now, as a servant.

Kenneth Bailey,[14] who lived in the Middle East for 20
years, describes the return as extremely improbable. The son
would likely have been killed upon arrival. Such churlish behavior would have never been tolerated by the community,
let alone by the father. Being accepted as a servant would
have been the ultimate act of grace and forgiveness from a
father abundant in mercy.

Recognizing his son from afar, the Father ran, therefore
shamelessly exposing his legs (girding His loins) by raising
his garments and welcomed the boy with arms wide open.

This action by the father took place because once the son returned to the community, he would have been seen as boorish and untreatable and would have very probably undergone the *kezazah* protocol[15] which would permanently exclude him from the community. The Father, by embracing the boy, spared his son but also submitted himself the punishment the son deserved.

When the son humbly confessed his sinfulness, stating he is *not worthy anymore*, as he once felt he was, the father had heard all He needed and lavished that son with all the symbols of true sonship—the finest robe, the ring, and a pair of sandals. The finest robe, usually kept for special occasions or for esteemed guests, likely belonged to the father himself. By draping it over his son, he openly restored his son's dignity and position in the family. This robe serves as a clear symbol that the son is not to be regarded as a servant or an outsider, but as a cherished and fully reestablished member of the household now robed in the Father's Righteousness.

The sandals the father placed on his returning son also carried profound symbolic meaning. Back then, only free members of a household wore sandals, while slaves typically went barefoot. Through this gesture, the father powerfully demonstrated his unconditional love and forgiveness, making it evident to everyone that the son's rightful place in the family had not changed

Not only was the son's place preserved, it was also elevated by his bearing the father's signet ring. While the text does not explicitly state that it was a signet ring, I put it to you that neither son had the ring at first. (We will discuss the signet ring in the next chapter.) Only after the boy returned and acknowledged he is not worthy anymore that he becomes fit to receive what the father bestows by grace. This is the culmination point at which the once-stray son finally understood what was at stake. The father's lavish bestowal of every sign of belonging—and, most importantly, authority—left the boy astonished, and at last beginning to discern the magnitude of his welcome.

Meanwhile, the older brother was inconsolable. If the younger brother had already taken his share and was now being welcomed back as a son—restored, no less, to honored standing—the older brother would naturally fear that his own inheritance would be diluted. From that angle, mercy could feel like loss, and restoration could seem indistinguishable from theft.

From a scarcity mindset, that welcome would have registered as theft. He might have thought, "That insolent brat already took his share; I want mine kept intact. But now I'm expected to absorb the cost—to make room for him out of what is rightfully mine." In a scarcity paradigm, blessing is always a zero-sum game: if another gains, someone else must lose.

But the father's act exposes how false that calculus is. The resources of the father are not precarious; his generosity is not measured out in fear. By reinstating the repentant son, he reveals a wealth that is not diminished by mercy.

Read theologically, the father reflects our Father—Righteousness, Justice, and Judge—who cannot act unfairly. His "estate" is not a limited cache of goods but an inexhaustible fullness of righteousness and life. Therefore, he can welcome a returning son again and again without ever nearing the edge of his true riches.

The older brother, chained to scarcity, remains furious and uncomprehending—blind to the real treasure that had been his all along —the estate of Life.

True Inheritance and Righteousness

"(…) buy from me gold refined in the fire, so you can become rich"

The inheritance in question is not merely monetary. The true treasure is that, God as the Judge, the ultimate authority in Justice, has given us His Spirit, the Witness, and Christ Himself, the Perfect Sacrifice and the Faithful Advocate, to show that the ultimate inheritance is in sharing in the Lord's Justice through its complete fulfilment and expression in Christ. In Christ we share in the full measure of His Justice. Every day we are called to be redeemed back unto Him through the Blood of Jesus so we might share in His perfect Righteousness and confess with the prophet: "YHWH, our Righteousness" (Jer 23:5–6).[16]

Paul nods to this reality when he states in Romans[17] that the Gentiles were wild olive shoots grafted into the cultivated olive tree. They will have royal, nourishing sap flowing through them, but they should bear in mind that this is not because of their original nature but by God's grace.

No matter how many sins we've left behind or how presumably holy our living is, we need to access that standard of Righteousness every day in order to remain in His Presence and expand His Kingdom as His representatives and regents here on earth. It's this continual drawing from His resources, not our own, that Jesus calls His people to in Revelation.

> *"I counsel you to buy from me* gold refined in the fire, so you can become rich; and *white clothes to wear, so you can cover your shameful nakedness; and*

salve to put on your eyes, so you can see." (Rev. 3:18, NIV emphasis added)

In this world, white garments do not remain spotless for long—unless they are continually cleansed by the Blood of the Lamb, who alone makes us "whiter than snow" (Isa 1:18; Ps 51:7; Rev 7:14) [18]. If we do not return to his Blood daily[19], we risk slipping into the posture of the older brother: presuming a standing before the Father grounded in merit.

But our merit is not ours. It is solely in Him.

Rewards that Last

The whole Bible is riddled with references to the reality that true wealth exists only in Him. "Blessed are the poor in Spirit, for theirs is the Kingdom of Heaven"[20] is the most explicit Jesus was in pointing to this reality. If we assume we are spiritually wealthy, believing our experiences have earned us special standing with God, or if we start to believe the praise (or flak) of others about our righteous lives (or shortcomings), we risk falling into the dangerous illusion that we have achieved some higher (or lower) spiritual status. In doing so, we deceive ourselves. Continually ascribing to God, and God alone, all Righteousness, Virtue, Praise and Value is a non-negotiable urgency.

If we do what we do in Him in order to accrue credit with people, we might be counted among those Jesus referred to as hypocrites.

"So when you give to the needy, do not announce it with trumpets, as the hypocrites do in the synagogues and on the streets, to be honored by others. Truly I tell you, *they have received their reward in full.*[21]

The word for "reward" in Greek[22] is used by Christ in Luke 6[23] in reference to the (great) reward for loving one's enemies, doing good and lending to others while expecting *nothing in return.* If repayment is demanded—whether from people or from God—repayment may indeed come; but it will be wages of a far lesser kind: *pennies* where the king offers *treasure.*

Once the younger brother spent whatever *reward* he generated himself, which is exactly what the father gave him, it dawned on him that what he was able to generate justice-wise was indeed minimal, evanescent, and fleeting. His words, "I'm not worthy to be called a son anymore, please treat me as a servant," points to the sobering[24] but beautiful realization that there is nothing else (self-generated) to his name. That feeling of entitlement is no more, and now, he is in the fitting sweet spot in which we are called to be found on a daily basis before the Father.

The father then lavished him with his authority and the returning boy's repentant posture implies what our daily response should be: "You are my Yahweh *Tsidkenu,* The Lord, Our Righteousness." The younger son is the sinner who repents, acknowledging he does not possess righteousness, and the older brother represents the 99 (self-)righteous who believe they need no repentance. And here Jesus gives voice to Heaven's own heartbeat: "I tell you, in the same way there will be more joy in heaven over one sinner who repents than over ninety-nine righteous persons who do not need to repent" (Luke 15:7).

6

THE SIGNET RING

SEVERAL OLD TESTAMENT SCENES SHOW rulers entrusting representatives with this authority by handing over their signet rings—often to people outside the royal family line. Joseph receives Pharaoh's signet[1] (Gen 41:42); Mordecai[2] receives Xerxes's ring that had been reclaimed from Haman (Esth 8:2); and Jezebel notoriously exploits Ahab's seal[3] to enact injustice (1 Kgs 21:8). The pattern is striking: a ring can be bestowed to delegate authority—or abused to counterfeit it.

Read spiritually, this becomes a warning as much as a wonder. Scripture repeatedly calls God's people to exercise authority only as stewards who continually return all glory to the true King. There is no place for entitlement here; there has always been—and will only ever be—one King[4] (cf. 1 Sam 8:6–7).

We are called to take on this beautiful regency[5] to act on His behalf. But would God hesitate to entrust us with His authority? On the contrary. He knows our hearts have a natural penchant towards independence and entitlement and is inviting us to dwell continually in this place where we credit all authority to Him alone. Bear in mind that a beautiful spiritual being once was His perfect signet. The king of Tyre (typologically read as satan) is described as having been the signet (*chotam*) of perfection[6] in Ezekiel 28. Nothing was lacking in this perfect being, but because the ultimate manifestation of Love is freedom, the Lord allowed the morning star to exercise his discretion. Having been ravished by an overwhelmingly cosmic sense of entitlement, the spiritual being succumbed to the temptation of believing that authority was his own.

The question, then, is: who bears the seal now? We cannot afford to succumb to the same trap of confusing delegated authority with ownership.

Chotam: The Biblical Signet

One of the Old Testament words used for a signet ring is *Chotam* (pronounced "hotam")[7]. It refers to signets on rings and cylinders used to leave an imprint on documents, making them official and pointing to their owner. To seal something was to claim it: it signaled ownership, legitimacy, and delegated clout; therefore, unauthorized tampering with sealed items was treated as a grave offense in the ancient world.

What then does it mean that we are sealed by God[8] with the promised Holy Spirit?[9] To say the least, no one, not a single entity who is not part of His kin is authorized to touch us. God has all our strands of hair counted[10] and cared for. Being sealed by the Spirit is not just a mark of belonging. It is also a sign of divine authority and protection. This principle becomes vividly clear in John's vision in Revelation. He wept because no one anywhere was found worthy to break the seals. Then one of the elders comforts him, telling him that the Lion of the Tribe of Judah, who had triumphed, was found worthy to open the seals. This points to the fact that Jesus, the Lion, shares the very same nature as God, which is not the same nature as all other entities who are unworthy to break the seals. The Lion of the Tribe of Judah has received the authority to bring into existence the decrees ordained by God Himself. Yes, and that authority is bestowed upon his regents, never as owners of it, but as those who bear His seal.

Signets aim to leave an imprint on material originally meant to be impermanent, namely wax or clay. In the combination of wax or clay with the seal, the latter dignifies the former. God's seal on us points to our current embodied state of existence as ephemeral. Yet through His seal, our true identity and purpose are made enduring, marked by His authority.

The concession of the signet ring to us also points to a central verse in Exodus. God ordained a signet to be worn by Aaron, the high priest, on his forehead with the inscription, *"Kodesh lAdonai"* —Holy to the Lord.[11] Yes, the same imprint on the signet ring on the cover of this book. This signet, or *chotam*, was to be worn as an expression that the mind of the high priest must be fully consecrated to the Eternal. It also signified that they are to leave imprints on everyone and everything surrounding them. Everything is to be presented with the possibility of being made holy unto the Eternal around all of us. Likewise, we are a Kingdom of priests,[12] called to influence the world around us, and, with our signets, leave imprints of consecration unto our Eternal Father for the expansion of His Kingdom.

The Prodigal Son and the Signet

Returning to the story of the repenting son, we see that he was given his father's signet ring to govern his realm, manage his estate, and command on his behalf. Christ portrays what the Father wants to communicate: His wealth is boundless. It is everlasting and inexhaustible. Just as the repentant son was given direct access to his father's realm and wealth, to manage it on his behalf, we are called to use the Father's resources to make of other unworthy children co-heirs of this never-ending wealth.

The father, by lavishing his son with the signet ring, communicates to both sons that:

1) The sons' entitlement and sense of self-worth used to be an insurmountable hurdle but isn't anymore—at least not for the younger one.

2) The father's estate is inestimable, infinite, and available to all repentant children who don't presume entitlement. The father would never divide the older son's portion no matter how hefty. That would have been a misalignment with the father's fairness. The father can be lavish with His giving because there is no end to His fortune.

3) The older son needs to understand this in order to enter into spiritual abundance.

Had the older son understood the depth of what was being articulated, he wouldn't have assumed he'd have to share of *his* portion with the returning brother. Honoring the younger son with the sign of highest honor and authority signifies that the Father's wealth is infinite, and no matter how many times one attempts to share it, it never diminishes.

Chotam Today

In January 2025, President Trump began his second term and, that same day, signed a series of executive orders in a scene staged for the cameras. The bold Sharpie strokes made the signatures conspicuous- built for photographs as much as for policy.

Had that moment been staged two millennia ago, the visual centerpiece would not have been a marker but a hefty signet ring. In my regular Hebrew study, I was struck to learn that *chotam* is the modern Hebrew word for "signature." Just last week, I *chotammed* an agreement—making my commitment binding and official—and it reminded me how the ancient logic of authorization by seal still carries spiritual resonance today.

The *chotam* does more than mark ownership; it legitimizes speech. Once the seal is applied, words become binding realities. The next chapter explores that binding power: decrees.

7

REGENTIAL DECREES

ABOUT FIVE YEARS AGO, I STARTED PRACTICING the writing of decrees—written statements issued with the intention of halting spiritual attacks on specific individuals. I learned this with a young gentleman named Kaisser[1] in Brazil. As people shared their challenging situations with me, I started exercising and honing this authority I already knew we have in the name of Jesus Christ.

Since then, I've received countless testimonies from people whose names were included in such decrees. One of the first times I exercised the use of decrees was for my chiropractor and trainer in Brazil. He told me that both his wife and daughter were mocking him because of his faith and because his business was faltering. I took the liberty of writing a decree in his favor, commanding the immediate suspension of all spiritual attacks on his wife and daughter that very day. I signed and dated the document, read it out loud, and saved it.

A couple days later, at our next session I asked him how things were at home. To my joy, he reported that his wife had started showing interest in the biblical teachings videos he'd been listening to. She even asked him to pray with her the night before. Only then did I tell him that I had written a decree on his behalf and showed it to him. We both thanked the Lord together and left the session immensely encouraged.

Another occasion arose while we were part of a Bible study group during our time in Berlin. One member shared that her husband had told her he was filing for divorce and planned to move to Africa to live with his mother. I asked her if she would allow me to prayerfully respond to this, and once she agreed, I asked for the names of the people involved.

After writing and signing the decree, I posted it in our group and asked all the members to pray and agree with the contents of the decree. Some four days later, she posted on the group chat that her husband had travelled back to Berlin and asked for her forgiveness. Additionally, he had started doing the dishes, which he had never done before, and told her that he would do anything if she would take him back, even going to church with her, which he had never done before. This was extraordinarily exciting because we all experienced the power we exert both individually and collectively as children of our spectacularly generous Father.

Identity over Technique

When exercising our authority, there is no recipe or technique to follow. As a spiritual scientist, I put biblical tenets to the test, and this was no different. Yes, we all love techniques. Every art in life is enhanced and more fully appreciated only after we develop certain techniques, so they are often useful, but not here.

This exercise of authority is an expression of our very identity as children of a loving Father. We receive authority as we continually worship Him, absorbing His Nature, Character, and His Name above all names. Nothing is ours by merit, and therefore, we must give all Glory and Honor back to Him—the source, sustainer, and fulfilment of everything in our lives. This practice has more to do with *who* we become in Him than *how* we do what we do.

Below is an example of a decree:

Place: Date: Time:
IDENTITY STATEMENT I, Daniel Gomma, son of the Most High, co-heir and co-regent with Christ, submit these words to the Father's will and Christ's lordship, and by His Grace and under His Authority I decree that:
Commands

1) **Immediate interruption of attacks** Every evil spirit, every unclean spirit, and every work of darkness operating against John Doe must cease now—immediately halt, immediately desist, and immediately lose all access and influence over his life, mind, body, and environment, in the Name of Jesus Christ.

2) **Expulsion of evil spirits (person and places)** I command every evil spirit afflicting or oppressing John Doe to depart at once and not return; and I command every evil presence, harassment, or spiritual contamination to be expelled from every place connected to him—his home, rooms, belongings, workplace (and/or place of

study), and daily routes—now, in the Name of Jesus Christ.

3) **Expulsion of disease and affliction** Every disease, infirmity, and affliction—whether physical, emotional, or psychological—assigned against John Doe: be expelled and broken off immediately and let his body and mind be restored to peace and wholeness, in the Name of Jesus Christ.

4) **End of confusion and harassment** Every spirit of confusion, fear, torment, intimidation, accusation, and disturbance sent against John Doe: stop now. Silence your voice, withdraw your pressure, and lose your power immediately, in the Name of Jesus Christ.

5) **Prohibition and separation** I decree a complete separation between John Doe and every evil assignment, monitoring, retaliation, and spiritual interference. No replacement, no regrouping, and no continuation of the attack is permitted, in the Name of Jesus Christ.

Final enforcement clause
May the above be immediately enforced by the Name of Jesus Christ, Amen!

Chotam,
Time:

Though this pattern is not meant to be a strict formula, it provides a foundational structure as you learn to exercise and articulate your own decrees.

Exercising the Signet of His Name

When Jesus taught us to pray and entreat in His Name, He was pointing to the dynamic of bearing and exercising His authority. To speak in His Name—as a worshipper of the Most High—is to bear His Name and Nature, His signet ring, and the Holy Spirit, the seal of God.

What I implemented in the decrees and in various prayers is this concept of exercising the use of His signet ring. It is the King Himself who guarantees the request, petition, entreaty, decree or command. I know this claim about the power and reality of His signet sounds startling, but please believe me—it is real. This seal, which needs no symbol, manifests and puts all other sigils (literally, lesser or little seals) to shame. All entities recognize true hierarchy, just like the centurion[2] in the Bible who immediately recognized real authority and power in Jesus. "But just say the word, and my servant will be healed. For I myself am a man under authority, with soldiers under me. I tell this one, 'Go,' and he goes; and that one, 'Come,' and he comes. I say to my servant, 'Do this,' and he does it" (Matthew 8:8–9 NIV). In the same way, every entity in the heavens—and beneath them—acknowledges that when we act in union with God, they are confronting the Lord Most High Himself; and at that reality they shake, tremble, and fear.

Notice how the focus is not on my accrued experience, any titles I might have, or how holy I have been (or failed to be). I first pray His Blood over me, and then I write the decree. I start by stating who I am. I then affirm who endowed me with such authority. Next, I issue the command and order its immediate enactment and enforcement in Christ's Name. I then agree with and *chotam* (seal) the decree. Finally, I rest and thank the Lord for carrying it through. Done.

Bear in mind what Jesus told us in Matthew 16:19: "I will give you the keys of the Kingdom of Heaven; whatever you bind on earth will be bound in heaven, and whatever you loose on earth will be loosed in heaven." The words "bind" and "loose" in Greek[3] refer to the common understanding that rabbis had the divine authority to allow and forbid certain practices. Jesus was communicating to His followers that they were being given the authority to govern on His behalf, by His Name. They once behaved as subjects in a prior realm but now were being invited into regency in His Kingdom.

Consider Peter exercising authority through a direct command: "In the name of Jesus Christ of Nazareth, walk" (Acts 3:6). Peter did not merely ask Christ to heal the man, nor did he pause to negotiate whether healing might be God's will in that moment; he spoke as one familiar with the King's courts and confident in delegated power.

Picture Joseph in Pharaoh's administration. Would he repeatedly seek permission to use the royal silos to store grain, or consult Pharaoh over the price of every sack sold? In the same way, we order, decree, and command in the Name above every name. As intimacy with Him deepens, the mind of Christ shapes our discernment, and we enforce what accords with His will.

This is a staggering level of trust: to be entrusted with His "assets," to steward what is His, to advance into contested territory—living under His continual confidence. God places weighty trust in us by granting access to His Name—His signet-ring authority. That is why, when someone asks whether God can be believed in, a startling answer might as well be this: it is God who has decided to place His trust in us.

8

THE POWER BEHIND A NAME

YEARS AGO, I ENCOUNTERED A LINE FROM Eugen Rosenstock-Huessy that stayed with me: a name is the "address" of speech. From that premise, much becomes plain in everyday life. I rarely respond to messages that are not directed to me personally; group messages often pass without reply. But when someone addresses me by name, I feel almost obligated to answer, and to ignore it seems—somehow—neglectful.

This also helps explain why unanswered mobile notifications can provoke anxiety: we are created to respond when addressed.

I trace this reflex, in part, to my relationship with God. When I address Him, He answers—sometimes by a nudge of insight, sometimes by silence, sometimes by the tangible gift of His Shalom. Both His nearness and silence are so steady that it makes me feel personally favored (and only He can do that for everyone, while it remains true). Because He meets me with that attentiveness, I find myself compelled to answer when others address me.

In this way, responsiveness becomes the soil from which responsibility grows. True responsibility emerges from knowing one's name and recognizing it being called—whether from within one's conscience or from without.

Names and the Spiritual Theatres of War

In the ancient world, those who knew the names of local deities used them in incantations in hopes of gaining leverage. These deities also had sigils, which were graphic signatures tied to their names, allowing those who dabbled with spiritual darkness to access a certain amount of power to secure their own ends.

Bear in mind that for most people who have ever existed, life unfolded under the shadow of spiritual darkness.[1] They had to learn to discern direction in a world of blurred shades. "The people walking in darkness have seen a great light; on those living in the land of deep darkness a light has dawned" (Isaiah 9:2) Had I lived in pitch-black times, would I have negotiated with any light bearer[2] to see anything at all, to try to make sense of it? Would you? How tremendously blessed are we that we are not bound by darkness and its endless traps anymore?

Darkness explores these precise dynamics of power. Some dark entities are more powerful than others, which lead their dark priests to feuds, showboating, and power plays. deities (yes, lower case "d" forever, even when starting a sentence) were allotted territories in the aftermath of the Tower of Babel. In Deuteronomy 32:8,[3] we see God dividing the nations and assigning their boundaries. The original wording indicates this was done "according to the number of the sons of God," pointing to a divine council framework.[4] Israel is eventually uniquely chosen as God's own inheritance, emphasizing its special significance within the biblical story.

Across the centuries, people in pagan religions—worship directed toward lesser powers—have been enticed into offering sacrifices to whatever entity was thought to preside over a given domain of life. The appeal of the deception is its promise of control: it invites a person to secure outcomes by feeding desire, flattering power, and bargaining for favor. As a result, its forms are as varied as human ambition. It can look like trying to purchase spiritual advantage for business, romance, or status, or like cultivating the patronage of a deity associated with war, the arts, political dominance, or even sex. The usual baits are power and fame.

The motto of the pagan/satanic movement is: *Do what you will. You want it? We've got your back.* Conversely, the motto of Christ is: Come and see how good and pleasant the will of God is for you and your beloved ones.[5] The spirit of witchcraft is ego-centric, self-serving, and manipulative. The Holy Spirit inspires and indwells, and the outcome is a manifestation in Kingdom living: it is for freedom that we have been set free[6]. And because we have been set free, we are called to set others free as well.[7]

Evocatio Deorum

The ancient world was well acquainted with this reality of spiritual territories. When nations went to war, there was a clear understanding that the clash was foremost a confrontation between deities and the realms under their dominion. Often, kingdoms would change their devotion to the gods of the victorious party or simply syncretize them into their pantheon. In fact, most ancient cultures deemed kings as being either gods themselves (Egypt most notably) or their direct representatives.[8]

The Roman rite of *evocatio deorum*[9] ("summoning deities") operated as a liturgy of empire expansion: Rome aimed to sap an enemy's strength by inviting the land's patron gods to consent to annexation, abandon their former cult site, and receive new sanctuary and honors in the capital—thereby ever enlarging Rome's pantheon. In the long run, this same logic of religious incorporation helped fertilize syncretism, as patterns of localized patronage were repurposed within later forms of devotion. The veneration of saints is one example of a cosmetic repurposing of ancient pagan practices.

Every major Roman martial campaign involved such *evocatio*, revealing the Romans' established conviction in a council of deities, and showing how placating their squeamish drives enabled them to conquer vast territories. This practice was one of the first expressions of the new world order, demonstrating spiritual agreement (if that is even possible) in the dark places. Seneca[10] was the first to call it *pax romana*—Roman peace—achieved by placating the whims of various territorial deities.

Pax Romana[13] was "peace" as the world gives: an externally enforced order, achieved by conquest, maintained by deterrence, and experienced by subject peoples as stability under an imperial ceiling. Jesus prepared His listeners,

---

[13] The Pax Romana ("Roman Peace") refers to a long period of relative stability across the Roman Empire, classically dated from Augustus (27 BCE–14 CE) to Marcus Aurelius (161–180 CE). It maintained "peace" largely through imperial control—law, taxation, military dominance, and the suppression of resistance—producing public order and security, but not necessarily inner wholeness or moral renewal.

warning them about such simulacrum of peace, when He stated: "Peace I leave with you; my peace I give you. I do not give to you as the world gives. Do not let your hearts be troubled and do not be afraid" (John 14:27 NIV). The known world back then was basically Rome and its neighboring client states, and the only peace they had to give was *pax romana*. Jesus' Peace is certainly not the *pax romana*, but rather the Cosmic Shalom. Thus, messianic Shalom is not an imperial quietness externally imposed, but a reconciling, barrier-breaking wholeness established from within, under the Prince of Peace Himself, the Sar Shalom[14].

Transactions of Darkness versus Relationship with Christ

In the pagan world, people constantly conjured the names of these gods who catered to people's whims and desires. There was a certain power available when a devotee acquired the right to call upon these deities. Gaining that access always came at a cost—usually money, or even life, through the shedding of blood. Darkness sells access to its power, and this always occurs through a transaction. People who meddle in darkness often used *sigils*[11] – the pictorial signatures of the entities ruling a certain region. A sigil communicated to other spiritual entities that the person had acquired the right to access them via that transaction, thereby entering into such authority.

---

[14] "For to us a child is born, to us a son is given, and the government will be on his shoulders. And he will be called Wonderful Counselor, Mighty God, Everlasting Father, Prince of Peace." Isaiah 9:6 NIV

The spiritual realm of darkness is governed by hierarchies who charge hefty prices to access their power only available in the jurisdiction of darkness. It is as if total darkness were selling lighter shades of itself. But now, who wants a hint of luminescence when Christ's glorious Light is available?

If in the pagan world, entities exchange their power through transactions, Christ, on the other hand, bestows His Power through relationship. I have experienced first-hand, several times, that:

1) Yes, dark entities have power, limited to the jurisdiction of darkness.

2) The powers of darkness simply dissolve at the Name of Jesus, and this terrifies them because mediums, dark priests, and everyone deceived by them learn that there is a certain "entity" unrivalled in power who commands immediate obedience and is so fearsome that His mere Name—spoken by a Name bearer—dissipates all confusion and lies, bringing Shalom, clarity, deliverance, and Love.

3) Those who meddle with the occult and attempt to harm followers of this "higher entity" quickly learn that these followers are inaccessible and untouchable, as long as they bear His Name and, by extension, His Nature. They maintain this protection by keeping themselves free from spiritual blots through Christ's Blood, clothing themselves in garments that are whiter than snow.

Darkness trembles in fear of their little secret
coming to light.[12] The bearer of the Name
who flirts with sin hides from the Father. The
bearer of the Name who dwells in the
Presence of the Father makes darkness flee in
fright.

While the *evocatio*[13] summons an entity to leave the territory about to be invaded, we, on the other hand, practice the *invocatio*[14] *Dei*, a summoning of the One and only Lord of Lords to indwell us. The *evocatio* aims to manipulate spiritual forces to adapt to the client's own will. The *invocatio Dei* invites us to submit to the will of this Loving God, who reassures us, as beloved children, that we can trust Him ever more. Because our God is neither forceful nor manipulative like other simulacra of gods, we must invoke Him daily and submit to His immense Love throughout our lives, one day at a time.

The difference between *evocatio deorum* and *invocatio Dei* is that in the former, the person wants everything for themselves. Over time, as we invoke God, we slowly discover that everything belongs to Him. When my youngest son learned to talk, he would say "It's mine!" all the time. In fact, he believed that everything was his. Maturity brings us the beautiful realization that nothing is ours. Everything belongs to the Father, and we are merely stewards of His possessions for His purposes.

Everything belongs to the Father, and we are merely stewards—handling His gifts for His purposes, and learning freedom in that continual relinquishment. If you question this reality, just ask someone who has written their will or is bidding their last farewell to life whether they were ever truly the owners of anything.

What I have shared above points to God's unequivocal supremacy and preeminence over entities that are very real, very powerful, but completely defenseless before Him. However, He is also the God of a very deep Love.

God's preeminent Love

A few months ago, while returning home by train after a day's work, I felt the tangible presence of God. As I sat meditating on Him, His love enveloped me in an extraordinary way. An elderly gentleman sat directly in front of me, and I clearly sensed that God wanted me to speak to him—to tell him about the love the Father felt for him. "But Father, how am I going to do this?" I thought.

The Father's presence grew even greater. I couldn't take it anymore[15]. I complimented him on the moss-green coat he was wearing. He responded in a friendly, modest way, saying it was already old. We exchanged a few words and introduced ourselves. Then I got straight to the point. I asked him if he knew that God had a very great, very deep love for him.

The crowded train faded away. It was just John and me. He was speechless, as if he wanted to say something but was overcome with emotion. His eyes welled up, and my whole being flooded with His indescribable love. "God sees you as a boy, extremely and profoundly loved," I concluded.

I heard my station being announced. I stood, said goodbye, and stepped off the train while still immersed in the

---

[15] " ...You anoint my head with oil; my cup overflows..." Psalm 23:5. When we overflow, we do so to fill other vessels—why would we squander this treasure?

Father's indescribable Love. I prayed for that man for some time, thanking the Father for the way He cares for us all. Only He knows why John needed that divine encounter. And only I know what I gained by obeying and taking a stand before Him.

Irrevocable love

In 2025, we witnessed the revocation of the noble titles of Prince Andrew, brother of King Charles of England. The process was painful to observe and unsettling for the country. Over the years, Andrew became associated with a notorious American pedophile, and later reports suggested involvement with Chinese interests, with the alleged intent of sharing privileged information. For the Crown, it became the final tipping point—drastic action followed.

For much of his life, his public identity appeared bound to royalty, almost inseparable from it. Yet when titles are stripped away, what remains is a man—simply Andrew. And here lies a sobering truth: human honor can be granted and withdrawn, but God's love cannot.

What an opportunity he now has—to return, to be humbled, and to rediscover himself in God: not overwhelmed by titles or a reputation, but as a soul whom the Father still calls and invites.

From time to time, the life of the church must address harmful or inappropriate behavior—sometimes even among leaders. This is what Christians have long called *discipline*: a necessary process meant to protect the community and heal what has been damaged. The challenge is to apply it in a way that confronts what must change without treating the person as disposable. Scripture's aim is restoration—"restore… gently"—not humiliation.

What often keeps people from returning is not merely the sin itself, but a lie that sin plants: that shame is final, that failure is unforgivable, that the door back to the Father has closed. When that lie takes root, a prodigal stops walking home. Yet returning to the Father is meant to be ordinary for believers—daily, even hourly—the steady rhythm of repentance and trust, like the tide's ebb and flow.

To hinder a brother or sister from returning to the Father's bosom is to adopt a merely human paradigm of righteousness: to make justice subjective, to replay the Pharisees' script, and to fall into the enemy's trap—namely, that our acts of righteousness earn the Father's favor. They never have, and they never will.

9

BEARING HIS NAME

GROWING IN FAITH IN BRAZIL ALLOWED FOR certain experiences that quickly made it clear that being a bearer of His Name (in practice, a user of His signet) comes with tremendous power over darkness. Brazil is riddled with expressions of darkness through the followers of the Brazilian version of *santeria*, namely *macumba* and its variants. One often sees offerings of food and alcohol at crossroads, and these religions still cater to those with a relentless drive to manipulate others. Witchcraft, simply put, is the religion of manipulation. Christ-bearing is the practice of freedom, the dwelling in liberty, a daily choice for Him.

When I still lived in Rio, I made the decision to praise Jesus every time I saw such offerings, whether in the forest, on the beach, or when driving past a religious store selling its paraphernalia. I knew deep inside that when I praised Him in such scenarios, I embarrassed the entities by reminding them of who will eternally receive all Honor, Glory and Praise from those redeemed by the Blood of the Lamb.

I used to jog on the Botafogo beach and because it was rather short, I'd cover it several times during my workout. On some occasions, I saw people placing their offerings on the beach. I'd pray and glorify God, stating that only He is worthy to be praised.

One day as I was running, I noticed a couple bringing two large bags towards the edge of the water. I immediately discerned they were about to make an offering to the deities deceiving them. By then, I had decided I would not rebuke any dark entities. I would simply pray the Spirit over the whole beach. When I saw them setting out the materials used for the offering on a cloth, I started praying that the Spirit would cover ever square meter of the beach. Without looking toward the couple again, I kept asking God to blow His Spirit over the whole area.

After a short while, I glanced at them again and saw they had packed their belongings and were hurrying towards the street. I'll never forget how they looked at me in fright, as if someone had told them I was a dangerous serial killer. God knows what lies they were told by the entities, but the couple was terrified. I only lament I didn't have a chance to share the Gospel with them, as I had before with several others deceived by this practice. Where the Spirit of the Lord is, there is Freedom indeed.[1]

If we choose to be known as being God-bearers, He expects us to take it seriously. Bearing His Name or wearing His signet in vain is publicly stating we are His while still intentionally meddling in sin, thereby forcing Him out of our lives. God cannot even contemplate evil; such is His Holiness. When we choose sin, even though God is Sovereign, He must withdraw from us[2] for His Light cannot coexist with darkness.

Imagine a conservative championing for abortive rights. Yes, an oxymoron. Bearing His Name in vain is also an oxymoron, living out expressions of darkness while stating we are His children. But when we take Him seriously and constantly call on Christ's Blood over our lives, God continually dwells in, over, and around us – and that makes darkness tremble in fear. Not because of us, but because of Him whose Nature we bear.

10

THE MIND: ANTECHAMBER OF REALITY

IN THE BEGINNING OF THIS BOOK, WE EXPLORED what it means to share in God's nature and how we constantly create reality through thoughts, words, and deeds. Our minds are holy ground, and our thoughts are the antechamber of reality. I treat the seat of my thoughts—my mind—as a literal space that I clean several times a day. I am constantly pleading the Blood of Christ over my mind, my eyes, my body, and my heart.

We do not enter the holiness that brings us into the King's chambers by moral strain or spiritual technique, but by His Blood first. From that place of access, worship draws us into communion, where we begin to absorb His Nature and grow into the portion of His image and likeness appointed for each one of us. This is deeply comforting, because I do not have to "measure up" in order to come near. I enter God through Christ—the flawless measure of perfection.

Taming Thoughts Before Taming the Tongue

As regents in the Kingdom of God, we are constantly creating realities, whether for good or bad. I learned that taming my tongue is an essential condition if I want to remain in Him. However, taming one's tongue comes after taming one's thoughts and before taming one's behavior.

Being a father of three beautiful children, I've found myself preoccupied with them in certain occasions. Once, when my older daughter was late from school, I had fleeting negative thoughts about possible reasons for her tardiness. Because I had realized that my mind is the antechamber of reality, I chose to have thoughts of peace instead, imagining her walking home joyfully, safe and sound. This simple exercise continually changed my whole internal setup.

There is no place for negative thinking or thoughts on violence, lust or deceit. If these thoughts intrude my mind—and trust me, sometimes they do—I immediately call on the Blood of Jesus and actively imagine the Lord's angels hovering around my dear ones with their swords of fire unsheathed, accompanying them wherever they go. I feel an immediate, lingering peace when I choose to generate these images.

These mental images are prayer in graphic form—the gestation of reality that, in due time, comes to term. Because what fills our minds inevitably shapes our speech, this practice overflows into the way I communicate. I don't badmouth myself or other people. Not because I feel *holier than thou*, but because I know I am not. Speaking well becomes second nature, and I constantly invite people around me to live in this same reality.

Many thinkers have deemed the mind an enemy. I wouldn't go that far, especially because it can and should be tamed, in order to bring forth life. The unconditioned mind works against us. A tamed mind, on the other hand, works wonders. Just like a garden is tamed wilderness or a working dog is a tamed animal, the mind, when tamed, enables magnificent realities to come to pass. For that to happen, we must have full dominion of it all the time. If I rule my inner dimension, I'll be ready to govern my surroundings.

Thermostats or Thermometers?

A couple weeks ago, while training a Jiu-Jitsu drill, my training partner that day justified not practicing that move on his left side because it was his "bad side." I invited him to never say that again and instead, as an alternative, call it the side that needs more attention. I could tell it immediately sank in.

We are designed to live this way—to pay attention to the inner dialogue that runs beneath our choices, and to take responsibility for it rather than letting it run unchecked. I practice this daily, and the result is both humbling and clarifying: whatever story I repeatedly tell myself becomes the world I end up inhabiting.

Here's the startling truth: in time, I will almost always prove myself right. If I keep telling myself I do things poorly, I rehearse mediocrity until it feels inevitable. But if I speak and believe that I can grow—if I affirm that I'm learning to do things with excellence and distinction—I begin to train my mind, habits, and expectations toward success.

A few months ago, while I was on a work trip, a colleague entered our meeting room complaining about the premises of the conference. Hearing others murmuring bothers me immensely, so I waited for a favorable moment and had a chat with her. I shared that we all have a super-power: *choice*. We can choose to be either *thermostats or thermometers*. We can choose to bring "good weather" wherever we go, or we can be ruled by life's ups and downs. She was ready for that reality, so I asked her if she would be interested in starting the conversation again, assuming dominion over how she responded to externalities. She did, and we all marveled. I saw her smiling for the rest of the week.

That same week, as we spoke about the many cultures represented, the subject of spirituality arose. Several of my colleagues expressed interest in the worldwide spread of Brazilian spirituality. As I explained that not every spiritual manifestation is positive even if very real, one of my colleagues shared that she was having terrible dreams with dark spiritual beings visiting her every night, robbing her of sound sleep and long-lost peace. I asked if she'd like to sleep like a baby that very night. She immediately smiled, saying that that was all she wanted.

We stepped outside for a brief talk, and I shared the Gospel. After I exposed the entities of darkness ruling the occult and its very real practices, we prayed together, and she renounced her involvement with tarot and palm reading. The following day, we met, and she couldn't hold her smile back. I asked how she had slept. "Like a baby!" she promptly answered in amazement. Such transformation points us back to a deeper reality: Our King intensely desires a reconnection with potential children, and we can and should take part in that.

I share these experiences to encourage you, my fellow regent in Christ, to boldly embrace this authority and walk out these realities as much as you possibly can.

11

FROM SUBJECTS TO REGENTS

THE KING'S INVITATION IS BOTH SIMPLE and staggering: will you serve as My regents until I return? Kingdom regency is not a costume we wear, but a life we receive—humble abiding in Him, attentive to His intentions, and steady with a royal posture before whatever the day brings. It is a calling to learn the arts of faithful living with curiosity and expectancy, trusting that each discipline will find its place as we carry out His commission.[1]

Regents are disciplined, interdependent, fast to learn and listen, and slow to speak. They practice taming the tongue[2] and are adept at learning Kingdom diplomacy. Regents know they are not kings, nor do they desire to take over that position from the One and Only King. They are fully dependent on the One they serve and love back. Knowing who covers them in their undertakings, they abide in the King's culture.

As regents absorb the King's nature, they are constantly surprised at what the King is able to do through them. Once joined in Him, they absorb His Nature and Character, reason with His mind, and exude His fragrance. Regents carry the

King's Victory and His undefeated Nature, understanding that earthly paradigms do not apply. The Kingdom often operates as an inversion—like a film negative—where what seems backward at first is simply waiting to be developed into full clarity

In this Kingdom, the paradigms invert. Victory is carried without triumphalism, authority is expressed through service, and honor is given away rather than demanded. Regents elevate others, celebrate the rising of their siblings, and refuse the petty rivalries of lesser courts; the household of regents becomes a living display of the King's wealth—many members, one body[3], each part rejoicing in the other's strength. They do not cling to titles, because their value does not depend on public recognition; it grows from within, rooted in the King's verdict over them.

Regents understand that sexual purity is an expression of the King's very nature. Once married, all other women and men are but siblings, and any other intimate relationship would be incestuous.

Regents know they were once subjects and do not live as entitled royals, but dialectally accept their new nature, absorbed by practicing daily worship of their King.

Together, let His regents say, "Come!"[4]

---

[1] מְלָכִים — *Melachim*: kings, reigning royals, monarchs

Introduction

[1] Rom 11:29 "…for God's gifts and his call are irrevocable."

Chapter 1

[1] [1]Then God gave the people all these instructions:

[2] "I am the Lord your God, who rescued you from the land of Egypt, the place of your slavery.

[3] "You must not have any other god but me.

[4] "You must not make for yourself an idol of any kind or an image of anything in the heavens or on the earth or in the sea. [5] You must not bow down to them or worship them, for I, the Lord your God, am a jealous God who will not tolerate your affection for any other gods. I lay the sins of the parents upon their children; the entire family is affected—even children in the third and fourth generations of those who reject me.[6] But I lavish unfailing love for a thousand generations on those[d] who love me and obey my commands.

[7] "You must not misuse the name of the Lord your God. The Lord will not let you go unpunished if you misuse his name.

[8] "Remember to observe the Sabbath day by keeping it holy. [9] You have six days each week for your ordinary work, [10] but the seventh day is a Sabbath day of rest dedicated to the Lord your God. On that day no one in your household may do any work. This includes you, your sons and daughters, your male and female servants, your livestock, and any foreigners living among you. [11] For in six days the Lord made the heavens, the earth, the sea, and everything in them; but on the seventh day he rested. That is why the Lord blessed the Sabbath day and set it apart as holy.

[12] "Honor your father and mother. Then you will live a long, full life in the land the Lord your God is giving you.

[13] "You must not murder.

[14] "You must not commit adultery.

[15] "You must not steal.

[16] "You must not testify falsely against your neighbour.

[17] "You must not covet your neighbour's house. You must not covet your neighbour's wife, male or female servant, ox or donkey, or anything else that belongs to your neighbour." (Exodus 20, NLT)

2 3 "Our God is in the heavens,
 and he does as he wishes.
4 Their idols are merely things of silver and gold,
 shaped by human hands.
5 They have mouths but cannot speak,
 and eyes but cannot see.
6 They have ears but cannot hear,
 and noses but cannot smell.
7 They have hands but cannot feel,
 and feet but cannot walk,
 and throats but cannot make a sound.
8 And those who make idols are just like them,
 as are all who trust in them.." Psalm 115:3-8 N:T
3 "The idols of the nations are merely things of silver and gold,
 shaped by human hands.
 They have mouths but cannot speak,
 and eyes but cannot see.
 They have ears but cannot hear,
 and mouths but cannot breathe.
 And those who make idols are just like them,
 as are all who trust in them "Psalm 135:15-18 NLT

4 "For God knew his people in advance, and he chose them to become like his Son, so that his Son would be the firstborn among many brothers and sisters." Romans 8:29 NLT

5 "As my glorious presence passes by, I will hide you in the crevice of the rock and cover you with my hand until I have passed byExodus 33:22 NLT

Chapter 2

1 https://en.wikipedia.org/wiki/Regent

Chapter 3

1 Drachon - δράκων in greek – also means *serpent*.

2 "If his good deeds had made him acceptable to God, he would have had something to boast about. But that was not God's way." Romans 4:2 NLT

3 ""Blessed are the poor in spirit, *for theirs is the kingdom* of heaven." Matt 5:3, emphasis added

4 I and Thou, page 114 of Kaufmann's translation; Ego says – I am like…

5 Theodrama: Theological Dramatic Theory / *"Theodramatik"*

Chapter 4

1 "You shall not intermarry with them, giving your daughters to their sons or taking their daughters for your sons, for they would turn away your sons from following me, to serve other gods. Then the anger of the Lord would be kindled against you, and he would destroy you quickly." Deut 7:3,4

2 https://www.goodreads.com/book/show/99007.Jewish_Literacy

3 Bearing in mind that we buy the field, not the treasure.

4 2 Cor 2:14-16

5 C.S. Lewis, *The Weight of Glory*: https://www.doxaweb.com/assets/weight_of_glory.pdf

6 "Blessed are the poor in spirit,
for theirs is the kingdom of heaven." Matthew 5:3

7 Shalom: completeness, soundness, welfare, peace.

8 "We are all infected and impure with sin.
When we display our righteous deeds,
they are nothing but filthy rags." Is 64:6

9 "I answered, "Sir, you know." And he said, "These are they who have come out of the great tribulation; they have washed their robes and made them white in the blood of the Lamb." Rev 7:14

10 "The Kingdom of Heaven is like a treasure that a man discovered hidden in a field. In his excitement, he hid it again and

sold everything he owned to get enough money to buy the field." Matt 13:44

11 "For just as the heavens are higher than the earth,
so my ways are higher than your ways
and my thoughts higher than your thoughts." Is 55:9

12 Matt 23:12 For those who exalt themselves will be humbled, and those who humble themselves will be exalted.

13 "For my people have done two evil things:
They have abandoned me—
the fountain of living water.
And they have dug for themselves cracked cisterns
that can hold no water at all!" Jer 2:13

14 "We now have this light shining in our hearts, but we ourselves are like fragile clay jars containing this great treasure.[a] This makes it clear that our great power is from God, not from ourselves." 2 Cor 4;7

15 https://traditionalkyoto.com/culture/kintsugi/

16 Saul was a Pharisee, belonging to the strictest sect of Judaism.; he was a "Hebrew of Hebrews" and a member of the tribe of Benjamin and held Roman citizenship, which afforded significant social privileges and the ability to travel freely across the Roman Empire. He was fluent in Koine Greek and Hebrew/Aramaic, enabling him to communicate with Jews and Gentiles alike, besides having been a notable leader, trained under Gamaliel.

17 "God chose the lowly things of this world and the despised things—and the things that are not—to nullify the things that are, 29 so that no one may boast before him." 1 Cor 1:28,29

Chapter 5

1 The word Kodesh in Hebrew means 'separated'

---

2 צְדָקָה — Tsedakah – Justice, righteousness, charity.

3 https://www.myjewishlearning.com/article/mitzvot-a-mitzvah-is-a-commandment/

4 "We are all infected and impure with sin.
   When we display our righteous deeds,
   they are nothing but filthy rags.
   Like autumn leaves, we wither and fall,
   and our sins sweep us away like the wind." Is 64:6 NLT

5 Matthew 13:44 "The Kingdom of Heaven is like a treasure that a man discovered hidden in a field. In his excitement, he hid it again and sold everything he owned to get enough money to buy the field."

6 In Luke 17:10, Jesus says: "So you also, when you have done everything you were told to do, should say, 'We are *unworthy servants; we have only done our duty'* (emphasis added).

7 "This made the Pharisees and teachers of religious law complain that he was associating with such sinful people—even eating with them!" Luke 15:2

8 The word "Pharisee" originates from the Aramaic *pərīšā* (פְּרִישָׁא), meaning "set apart" or "separated," which is related to the Hebrew *parush* (פָּרוּשׁ), the passive participle of the verb *parash* (פָּרַשׁ) meaning "to separate".

9 "In the same way, there is more joy in heaven over one lost sinner who repents and returns to God than over ninety-nine others who are righteous and haven't strayed away (*don't need to repent, in Greek*)!" Luke 15:7

10 Luke 15:8–10

11 Μισθός / *misthos* – reward, wages, recompense

12 "When you give to someone in need, don't do as the hypocrites do—blowing trumpets in the synagogues and streets to call

attention to their acts of charity! I tell you the truth, they have received all the reward they will ever get." Matthew 6:2

13 "Be happy about it! Be very glad! For a great reward awaits you in heaven. And remember, the ancient prophets were persecuted in the same way."

14 https://www.kennethbailey.net/about

15 The "*kezazah*" protocol refers to a ceremony describing the ancient Jewish practice, particularly surrounding the story of the Prodigal Son in Luke 15. The word "kezazah" comes from the Hebrew root *katzatz* (קצץ), meaning "to cut off." In these interpretations, the ceremony is a communal act designed to formally ostracize or "cut off" a Jewish person who had squandered his inheritance among Gentiles and attempted to return to his community.

16 "For the time is coming,"
says the Lord,
"when I will raise up a righteous descendant[a]
    from King David's line.
He will be a King who rules with wisdom.
    He will do what is just and right throughout the land.
6 And this will be his name:
    The Lord Is Our Righteousness.'[b] יְהוָה צִדְקֵנוּ
In that day Judah will be saved,
    and Israel will live in safety." Jer 23:5,6

17 Romans 11:11-31

18 "Come now, let us reason together, says the Lord: though your sins are like scarlet, they shall be as white as snow; though they are red like crimson, they shall become like wool." Is 1:18

"Purge me with hyssop, and I shall be clean; wash me, and I shall be whiter than snow." Psalm 51:7

19 have washed their robes and made them white in the blood of the Lamb" Revelation 7:14

20 Matthew 5:3

21 Matthew 6:2, emphasis added

22 *Μισθός*- misthos - reward, wages, pay, price, wage

23 "Love your enemies! Do good to them. Lend to them without expecting to be repaid. Then your reward from heaven will be very great, and you will truly be acting as children of the Most High, for he is kind to those who are unthankful and wicked." Luke 6:35

24 "Do everything they say to you," the Lord replied, "for they are rejecting me, not you. They don't want me to be their king any longer." 1 Sam 8:7

"But when you were afraid of Nahash, the king of Ammon, you came to me and said that you wanted a king to reign over you, even though the Lord your God was already your king." 1 Sam 12:12

Chapter 6

1 "Then Pharaoh removed his signet ring from his hand and placed it on Joseph's finger. He dressed him in fine linen clothing and hung a gold chain around his neck." Genesis 41:42

2 " The king took off his signet ring, which he had reclaimed from Haman, and presented it to Mordecai. And Esther appointed him over Haman's estate." Esther 8:2

3 "So she wrote letters in Ahab's name, sealed them with his seal (*chotam*), and sent them to the elders and other leaders of the town where Naboth lived." 1 Kings 21:8

4 But when they said, "Give us a king to lead us," this displeased Samuel; so he prayed to the Lord. 7 And the Lord told him: "Listen to all that the people are saying to you; it is not you they have rejected, but they have rejected me as their king" 1 Sam 8:6,7

[5] Regency refers to the period or office when a regent governs in place of a monarch who is unable to rule due to youth (being underage), absence, or incapacity (such as illness).

In the Kingdom of God, Regency takes on a wondrous, intimate meaning: God, ever-present and all-powerful, graciously invites us—His beloved children—into the joy of sharing in His Authority, co-reigning with Christ as faithful stewards of His eternal rule.

[6] "You were the signet of perfection, full of wisdom and perfect in beauty." Ez 28:12 חוֹתֵם תָּכְנִית (signet of perfection)

[7] חוֹתָם Chotam, seal, signet ring.

[8] " and who has also put his seal on us and given us his Spirit in our hearts as a guarantee."2 Cor 1:22

"But God's firm foundation stands, bearing this seal: "The Lord knows those who are his," and, "Let everyone who names the name of the Lord depart from iniquity." 2 Tim 2:19

"They were told not to harm the grass of the earth or any green plant or any tree, but only those people who do not have the seal of God on their foreheads." Rev 9:4

"Saying, "Do not harm the earth or the sea or the trees, until we have sealed the servants of our God on their foreheads." Rev 7:3

[9] "In him you also, when you heard the word of truth, the gospel of your salvation, and believed in him, were sealed with the promised Holy Spirit," Ephesians 1:13

[10] "But even the very hairs of your head are all numbered. Do not fear therefore; you are of more value than many sparrows." Luke 12:7; ""But the very hairs of your head are all numbered." Matt 10:30

[11] "Next make a medallion of pure gold, and engrave it like a seal with these words: Holy to the Lord." Exodus 28:36

12 "and you shall be to Me a kingdom of priests and a holy nation.' These are the words that you shall speak to the sons of Israel." Ex 19:6

"But you are a chosen race, a royal priesthood, a holy nation, a people for God's own possession, so that you may proclaim the excellencies of Him who has called you out of darkness into His marvelous light;" 1 Peter 2:9

"and He has made us to be a kingdom, priests to His God and Father—to Him be the glory and the dominion forever and ever. Amen." Rev 1:6

"You have made them to be a kingdom and priests to our God; and they will reign upon the earth." Rev 5:10

1 https://kaisser.me

Chapter 7

2 "But just say the word, and my servant will be healed. For I myself am a man under authority, with soldiers under me. I tell this one, 'Go,' and he goes; and that one, 'Come,' and he comes. I say to my servant, 'Do this,' and he does it." (Matthew 8:8-9)

3 "Bind" (δήσῃς, from δέω): to forbid to declare not allowed. Loose" (λύσῃς, from λύω): to permit to declare allowed.

Chapter 8

1 "The people walking in darkness
have seen a great light;
on those living in the land of *deep darkness*
a light has dawned." Is 9:2

2 Lucifer meaning: bearer of light.

3 When the Most High assigned lands to the nations,
when he divided up the human race,

he established the boundaries of the peoples
according to the number in his heavenly court.

4 https://biblehub.com/q/what_is_the_divine_council_concept.htm

5 "Don't copy the behaviour and customs of this world, but let God transform you into a new person by changing the way you think. Then you will learn to know God's will for you, which is good and pleasing and perfect." Romans 12:2

6 " It is for freedom that Christ has set us free. Stand firm, then, and do not let yourselves be burdened again by a yoke of slavery" Galatians 5:1

7 It's been said that a wounded person wounds, and a healed person heals.

8 Henri Frankfort's "Kingship and the Gods"

9 https://danielgomma.wixsite.com/daniel-gomma/post/the-triumph-of-the-victor

10 The Younger, in 55 AD.

11 sigil(n.) "a sign, mark, or seal," mid-15c., sigille, from Late Latin sigillum, from Latin sigilla (neuter plural) "statuettes, little images, seal," diminutive of signum "identifying mark, sign

12 A light switch brings light into a dark room, and there is no negotiating that light overrides of darkness, except when freewill is used to hinder this natural course.

13 From the Latin *evocare*, meaning "to call" or "to summon".

14 From Latin *invocare*, meaning "to invoke, appeal to or call upon." It is a Latin noun of the third declension (*invocatiō, invocatiōnis*), meaning "an invocation" or an act of summoning or invoking.

Chapter 9

1 "Now the Lord is the Spirit, and where the Spirit of the Lord is, there is freedom." 2 Cor 3:17

2 "But you are pure and cannot stand the sight of evil.
Will you wink at their treachery?" Hab 1:13

Chapter 11

1 "18 Then Jesus came to them and said, "All authority in heaven and on earth has been given to me. 19 Therefore go and make disciples of all nations, baptizing them in the name of the Father and of the Son and of the Holy Spirit, 20 and teaching them to obey everything I have commanded you. And surely I am with you always, to the very end of the age."" Matt 28:18-20

2 James 3

3 "12 The human body has many parts, but the many parts make up one whole body. So it is with the body of Christ. 13 Some of us are Jews, some are Gentiles,[c] some are slaves, and some are free. But we have all been baptized into one body by one Spirit, and we all share the same Spirit.[d]

14 Yes, the body has many different parts, not just one part. 15 If the foot says, "I am not a part of the body because I am not a hand," that does not make it any less a part of the body. 16 And if the ear says, "I am not part of the body because I am not an eye," would that make it any less a part of the body? 17 If the whole body were an eye, how would you hear? Or if your whole body were an ear, how would you smell anything?

18 But our bodies have many parts, and God has put each part just where he wants it. 19 How strange a body would be if it had only one part! 20 Yes, there are many parts, but only one body. 21 The eye can never say to the hand, "I don't need you." The head can't say to the feet, "I don't need you."

---

[22] In fact, some parts of the body that seem weakest and least important are actually the most necessary. [23] And the parts we regard as less honorable are those we clothe with the greatest care. So we carefully protect those parts that should not be seen, [24] while the more honorable parts do not require this special care. So God has put the body together such that extra honor and care are given to those parts that have less dignity. [25] This makes for harmony among the members, so that all the members care for each other. [26] If one part suffers, all the parts suffer with it, and if one part is honored, all the parts are glad.

[27] All of you together are Christ's body, and each of you is a part of it." 1 Cor 12:12-27

[4] "The Spirit and the bride say, "Come." Let anyone who hears this say, "Come." Let anyone who is thirsty come. Let anyone who desires drink freely from the water of life." Rev 22:17